o[illegible] St Anthony of Padua

Compiled and introduced by
Don Mullan

First published in 2003 by
the columba press
55A Spruce Avenue, Stillorgan Industrial Park,
Blackrock, Co Dublin

Designed by Bill Bolger
The cover picture is a detail from *The Christ Child Adored* by Kotignola, used by kind permission of the National Gallery of Ireland
Origination by The Columba Press
Printed in Ireland by
ColourBooks Ltd, Dublin

ISBN 1 85607 410 2

To

Dermot and Maureen Beatty

and to the memory of

Charles and Sara Mullan

Acknowledgements:

The publisher and editor gratefully acknowledge the permission of the following to quote from material in their copyright: Edizioni Messaggero Padova, Italy, for quotations from *If you seek miracles – Reflections of Saint Anthony of Padua* by Claude M. Jarmak, OFM Conv; www.franciscan-archive.org for quotations from *The Sermons of St Anthony*, translated by Fr Paul Spilsbury; Editions du Signe for quotations from *Anthony of Padua – Proclaimer of the Gospel* by Fr Lothar Hardick, OFM, translated by Fr Zachary Hayes, OFM, and Fr Jason M. Miskuly, OFM.

Author's Acknowledgements

Sincere thanks are owed to the following for their kind support and assistance with this publication:

Gary Burke, RIP, who departed this life on 7 March 2003; to Frank Burke and A Gift of Roses Trust for their openness and support; Fr Peter Rodgers, OFM Cap, who gave me the idea for this book; Bernie Bergin for her assistance with parallel reading and great goodwill, humour and friendship; John Ryan and his daughter Emer for editorial assistance; Fr Francis Cotter, OFM and Fr Finian Roche OFM for their very helpful guidance and encouragement; Fr Mario Conte, Editor, *Messenger of Saint Anthony*, Padua, Italy, for his great kindness; Brian Cushen, Merchant's Quay; and Eileen O'Callaghan of the Assisi Book Shop, Merchant's Quay, Dublin, for her great patience and support; to Seán O Boyle and the entire staff of Columba Press; Seamus Cashman who planted the seed of this Little Book series; and last but not least, my family: Margaret, Thérèse, Carl and Emma for their continued kindness and warmth.

Introduction

Fr Peter Rogers, Minister Provincial of the Franciscan Capuchins of Ireland, informed me during a meeting in Dublin in February 2003 that St Anthony of Padua was the most popular of all the Franciscan saints. He is more popular even than St Francis of Assisi!

Having aroused my curiosity I went in search of a saint whom I knew only as the finder of lost objects. I was, quite literally, amazed by the treasure trove of wisdom I found from the volumes of sermons he wrote and which the Franciscan Order has reverently preserved.

Anthony was born sometime between 1188 and 1195 in Lisbon, Portugal. He was baptised Fernando, a name meaning 'bold fighter for peace'. It is known he had a deep compassion for the poor.

He initially studied for the priesthood with the Canons Regular of St Augustine in the cloisters of Sao Vincent de Fora and the great monastery of Santa Cruz located at Coimbra, then the capital city of Portugal. Santa Cruz had a library stocked with the works of Augustine, Ambrose, Bede the Venerable, Gregory the Great, Isidore of Seville and many others. In time, Anthony would be considered their equal.

In 1220, however, Anthony decided to join the new order of brothers and priests founded by St Francis of Assisi. In 1223 St Francis directed Anthony to teach theology to members of the order in Bologna.

Anthony was a missionary in Morocco and later preached extensively in southern France and throughout Italy to huge crowds. In 1230 he began composing his *Sermones* for feastdays. Most of the quotations in this little book are taken from his sermons. He died on June 13, 1231, and was buried in the Church of Mary, Holy Mother of God, Padua, four days later.

Pope Gregory IX called him the 'Ark of the Testaments' and 'Repository of Holy Scripture'. In 1946 Pope Pius XII raised St Anthony to the status of Doctor of the Church.

Don Mullan
Dublin
7 April 2003

Quotations from St Anthony of Padua

St Anthony's Brief

Behold the Cross of the Lord!
Be gone you enemy powers!
The lion of the tribe of Juda,
the root of David has conquered, Alleluia!

I ask that
if you find anything edifying,
anything consoling,
anything well presented,
that you give all praise and glory
and all honour
to the Blessed Son of God, Jesus Christ.

If, on the other hand,
you find anything that is ill composed,
uninteresting or not too well explained,
you impute and attribute it
to my weakness, blindness,
and lack of skill.

Nature herself teaches us a lesson
in enclosing the tongue.
The teeth and the lips
were placed to safeguard the tongue
from uttering a word
without great caution.

Attribute to God
every good that you have received.
If you take credit for something
that does not belong to you,
you will be guilty of theft.

Deeds without devotion
are like a lamp without oil.

Good deeds

In the light of eternal life,
all our deeds are useless
unless they are tempered
with the balm of love.

Material Things

Solicitude for material things
distracts the soul and divides it.
The devil seizes the divided soul
and drags it to hell.

Material Things

Earthly riches are like a reed:
its roots sunk in the swamp
and its exterior is fair to behold,
but inside it is hollow.
If a man leans on such a reed
it will snap off and pierce the soul.

Material Things

Damned money!
Alas! How many religious did it blind!
How many cloistered religious
did it deceive!
Money is the 'dropping of birds'
that blinded the eyes of Tobit.
(Tob 2:10-12)

Repentance

If you offend or hurt Christ
by sinning grievously,
as soon as you offer
a flower of repentance,
he immediately forgets the offence,
forgives you the sin
and hurries to embrace and kiss you.

Forgiveness

If God, the Lord of our Creation,
forgives us so much,
why cannot we forgive one another
so little?

The Kingdom of God

We ought to seek the kingdom of God
and its justice above everything else.
Worldly-minded people
primarily seek material things,
and only afterwards
do they seek the things that are of heaven.

We should begin with heaven
for 'where our treasure is found,
there you will find our hearts
as well as our requests.'

Greed

Greed for money and power
can be compared to a fire
that never says 'enough'.
Instead it keeps on shouting:
'Give me more.'

Faith

A fish is not hurt
by the constant pounding
of the waves of the sea.
Neither is faith destroyed
by life's adversities.

The Cross

We look at the Crucified
and see the image of our Redemption.
Perhaps this sight will produce in us
a certain amount of suffering, albeit small.
However, as soon as we look away,
we divert our hearts to other things
and return to vain worldly amusements.

The Cross

Extending his arms on the cross like wings,
Christ embraces all who come to him
sheltering them in his wounds.

Peace

You ought to have eternal peace
with your neighbour,
internal peace within yourself
and internal peace with God in heaven.

Night

Night, which blinds the eyes,
represents mortal sin,
which obscures the light of reason.

Bodily senses

Sinners love their bodily senses
like brothers;
good people treat them as servants.

The sin of Adam

The sin of Adam was the destruction
and weakening of the human race.
It consisted in three things,
greed, vainglory and avarice.

Contrition

Contrition of the heart,
which illumines the soul,
makes us conscious of God,
of our own weakness,
and teaches us
to distinguish good from evil.

Confession

Confession ought to be 'uninhabitable'
like a desert,
private, secret, hidden
from everyone's knowledge,
and enclosed in the mind solely
of the confessor
under the inviolable seal of confession.

The Confessor

Even if everyone on earth knows the sin,
which the sinner confessed,
the confessor nonetheless would still have
to keep it sealed within himself
with the key of eternal silence.

Listen

O deaf one,
perk up your ears like the deer
and listen to the voice of your master
to recognise the cunning tricks
of the hunter-devil.
If you close your ears and refuse to obey,
believe me, you will be killed.

Constant soul

The darkness of the devil's temptation
will not put out the light
of the constant soul.

God will grow more and more in you
if you grow lesser and lesser in yourself.

Humility

Humility is the most noble of all virtues
because due to its nobility
it patiently endures things
that are less noble.

Humility

The spirit of humility
is sweeter than honey,
and those who nourish themselves
with this honey
produce sweet fruit.

Humility

If you wish to follow
you must leave yourself behind.
A person who follows another
looks not to the self
but to the other who is the leader.

Mystery of the Eternal Plan

O the gentleness of divine mercy,
O the patience of the Father's goodness,
O profound and inscrutable mystery
of the eternal plan!

What more can we say?

Today the earth is painted
with colourful roses and lilies.
Today the angels sing:
'Glory to God in the highest.'
Today, peaceful quiet
has returned to the earth.
What more can we say?

Everything rejoices

Everything smiles! Everything rejoices!
The angel announces to the shepherds:
'I come to proclaim good news to you,
tidings of great joy
to be shared by the whole people:
This day in David's city
a Saviour has been born to you,
The Messiah and Lord!'

Simplicity

O splendid gold of poverty!
Who does not possess you,
even though he has everything else
possesses nothing!
Material possessions inflate us
thus creating a void.
Simplicity brings joy.
Wealth, on the other hand,
brings worry and grief.

Whoever wishes to give solace
to one who is sick
must himself feel and participate
in that illness.

Helping Others

You will not be able
to carry another's burden
unless you first lay aside your own.
Unburden yourself first
to be able to carry another's.

Helping the Poor

Like the almond tree
blooms before all the others,
so must helping the poor
take precedence over all other acts
of a follower of Christ.

Love

Love is essential,
so that without love
all our efforts are in vain,
no matter how much good we accomplish.

The malice of a cold heart
is set alight by the fire of charity,
when he who hates is loved,
when he who persecutes
is given gifts in return.

The Just Man

The life of the just man
is compared to an instrument of music.
The musical instrument
is the word of gospel preaching
the melody of good repute
harmonising with a holy life.

The Just Man

From such a life
comes a sweet scented memory
that delights the minds
of those who hear,
as it sounds sweetly in their ears.

Prayer

Prayer is an expression
of a person's love for God,
a devout and familiar conversation,
an abandonment of a soul,
illumined by grace to enjoy the Lord.

In the life of the spirit
a 'petition' is an anguished and insistent
cry to God.

Prayer
is a pious and familiar conversation
with the Lord,
a conversation focused on God,
a restful sojourn with the Lord,
as much as this is possible.

Anger

When a man burns with anger
he is like a raging sea
because there is bitterness in his heart,
disturbance in his reason,
blindness in his mind
and rancour against his brother.

Salvation

If anyone finds himself
in danger of death
or in dire circumstances,
and is told that help is imminent,
would that person not smile and rejoice?
Indeed he would.

In the same way,
we ought to rejoice and be glad,
'for a Saviour has been born to us today
who will save us
from the power of the devil
and the prison of hell.'

The Saints

The saints are like stars …
Christ conceals them in a hidden place
so that they might not shine
before their time…
but they are always there,
ready to do so.

The Saints

The birds are the saints,
who fly to heaven
on the wings of contemplation,
who are so removed from the world
that they have no business on earth.

The Rainbow

Behold the rainbow!
Then bless its Maker!
It is beautiful in its splendour!

The Rainbow

It spans the heavens
with its glory,
bent by the hand of God!
(Sir 43:12)

Praise

The great thing is not to be praised,
but to be praiseworthy!

Actions speak louder than words;
let your words teach
and your actions speak.

The Holy Trinity

The Holy Trinity

There is one God the Father,
from whom we exist.
There is one God the Son,
through whom we exist.
There is one God the Holy Spirit,
in whom we exist.

The Holy Trinity

The Father is the font
and source of our existence;
the Son is the 'form', the exemplar,
which we are to follow,
and the Holy Spirit is the grace
which reconciles us to God.

The Holy Trinity

Praise be to the invisible Father,
Praise be to the Holy Spirit,
Praise be to the Son, Jesus Christ,
Lord of heaven and earth. Amen.

God the Father

God the Father

Our Father,
like a poor hungry beggar,
is knocking at our door
so that we may open it and give him,
if not a supper,
at least a small morsel of bread.

God the Father

No one can be called a father
except a person who has a child,
since these two words, 'father' and 'child',
are relative terms.
Thus, when you use the word 'Father',
you immediately think of a 'child'.
God is our Father and we are his children.
This is why we daily say 'Our Father'.

You saw, O Father,
your only begotten Son,
co-equal to you,
bound to a pillar like a criminal;
how could you restrain yourself?

We thank you, Holy Father,
because the chains and scourges
of your beloved Son
have freed us from the chains of sin
and the scourges of the devil.

Do not, O Lord, look upon our sins,
but rather look at the face of Christ,
covered with spittle,
swollen with bruises and tears
shed on account of our sins
to reconcile us sinners to you.

Christ shows his bruised face to you,
Lord, so that you may look at him
and, seeing it, you may be merciful to us
who were the cause of
his suffering and his passion.

We offer you thanks, O Holy Father,
For in the midst of winter,
in the midst of bitter cold,
you made springtime blossom for us.

With the birth of your Son,
the Blessed Jesus,
celebrated in the middle of winter
and amidst bitter cold,
you have given us a delightful breath
of the warmth of spring.

Look at the face of your Christ!
Is there a Father who would not
look at the face of his dead son?
Therefore, O Father, look at us,
because your Son, Christ, died for us,
who were the cause of his death!

Since he himself told us
to ask you in his name,
we beg you to give yourself to us,
because without you we cannot exist.

God the Son

Jesus

Jesus treats us
as lovingly and tenderly
as any mother who loves her child.

Jesus

When I behold my God
with the eyes of faith,
my spouse, my Jesus hanging on the cross,
pierced with nails,
his thirst quenched with gall and vinegar,
crowned with thorns,
then all the world's glory, honour
and fleeting pomp
pales to nothing and becomes worthless.

Jesus

Let us ask Jesus Christ
to fill us with his mercy,
so that we may practise compassion
with ourselves and others,
not judging nor condemning,
but forgiving those who hurt us
and helping those who are in need.

Help him then, brother,
help Jesus,
because if you become a sharer
in his trials,
you will also share in his consolations.

We ask you, Lord Jesus Christ,
who have ascended in our human nature
from this world to the Father
that you draw us after yourself
with the cord of your love.

We beg you not to accuse us of our sins,
to assist us in imitating
the holiness of the saints,
to stand in awe of your judgment.

May you infuse into us the Spirit of truth
who will teach us all truth.

May you who are blessed and glorious
throughout all ages,
grant us what we ask.
Let every soul say Amen! Alleluia!

May all praise, all glory, all honour
be given to the Son of God,
who is blessed, glorious for all ages.
May the whole church exclaim:
Amen! Alleluia!

To you, beloved Son of the Father,
the source of all good,
to you be all praise, all glory, all reverence.
You are the alpha and the omega,
the beginning and the end of all things.

May praise be given
to the invisible Father, to the Holy Spirit,
may praise be given to his Son,
Jesus Christ,
the Lord of heaven and earth. Amen.

O Son of God,
remember your poverty,
since even in death
you did not have a shroud of your own
in which to be wrapped,
nor a tomb of your own
in which to be buried.
These were given to you
as alms given to a poor beggar
out of mercy and kindness.

Lord Jesus Christ!
By your humility,
uproot the hypocrisy of our pride.
By your poverty,
drive out greed from our hearts.
By your patience,
destroy our anger.

By your obedience
during your sufferings and passion,
repress our disobedience.
With your help
may we always rejoice in you,
who are blessed throughout all ages.
Amen.

Lord Jesus,
make of us good and fertile soil,
for the reception of
the seed of your grace,
and make it yield worthy fruits
of penance,

so that with your help
we may merit to live eternally
in your glory,
who are blessed throughout all ages.
Amen.

The Holy Spirit

The Holy Spirit is:

The Fire of God,
The Dew of Light,
The Teacher of Truth,
The River of Fire,
The Spirit of Truth,
The Perfect Harpist of Israel,
The Spouse of the Soul,
The Omnipotent Word.

The Spirit cannot be seen
except through the acts of the person
within whom he is operating.

Reflect on this:
a fire brings down things that stand tall,
bonds together things that are disparate,
exposes things that are concealed,
penetrates things that are impenetrable,
moves constantly, always upwards,
away from the earth,
and finally it completely envelopes
anything that it touches with its flames.

These seven properties of fire
can be applied to the seven gifts
of the Holy Spirit.

The Holy Spirit

Fire has four properties:
it burns, purifies, warms and illumines.
In the same way the Holy Spirit
burns out sins, purifies hearts,
eradicates the coldness of apathy
with his warmth
and illumines minds.

The Holy Spirit

Let us speak
as the Holy Spirit
gives us the grace to speak,
humbly and devoutly imploring him
to infuse his grace
so that we may fulfil the days of
Pentecost.

The Holy Spirit

Note that with good reason is
the Holy Spirit called the Dew of Light.
Dew because he refreshes,
and light because he illumines.
When the Dew of Light enters the soul,
people who are dead because of their sins,
now live the life of grace,
and those, slain by the sword of their vices,
rise in the first resurrection
which is penance.

The Holy Spirit

Just as the human spirit
is the life of the body,
in the same way this Divine Spirit
is the life of the soul.
The former gives sensitive life,
the latter provides sanctifying life.

The Holy Spirit

He is called the Holy Spirit
because without him
no spirit, whether it be angelic or human,
can become holy.

The Holy Spirit

Happy is the man
whose words come from the Holy Spirit
and not himself.

May he who poured out his grace
on the apostles at Pentecost
as tongues of fire,
deign also to pour his grace into us.
To him be praise and glory always
throughout all the ages. Amen.

Holy Spirit, fire of love,
come rest over each of us,
make our tongue ready to confess our sins,
that in revealing everything
and concealing nothing,
we may attain heavenly life
to sing eternal praise with the angels.
With your help, you who live and reign
through all ages. Amen.

The Mother of God

Mary is like a moon resplendent in the glory of its fullness because she is perfect in every way … The glorious Virgin did not have any imperfections, whether in her birth since she was sanctified in her mother's womb and guarded by angels, nor during her lifetime because she never sinned by pride. She was always resplendent in the perfection of her life.

The Blessed Mother

O the boundless dignity of Mary!
O the ineffable sublimity of grace!
O the profundity of unplumbed mercy!
Was ever such a grace or such largess
given to any angel or human being
as was bestowed on the Blessed Virgin,
whom God the Father willed to be
the mother of his Son,
equal to him and born before all ages?

Let each and every one of us
raise our voices in praise
of the Blessed Mary
and call out to her son:
'Blest is the womb that bore you
and the breasts that nursed you.'

Let us laugh and rejoice
with the Blessed Virgin Mary
for God has given us cause for laughing
and rejoicing in her.

Thank you, O glorious Virgin,
for it is through your merits
that God is with us.
O Mary! You are a throne
in which sits the glory of the Father.

On this throne,
Jesus Christ took his place,
who lived among us on this earth
in our flesh.
Glory itself,
greater than any of the angels!

You, blessed Mary,
became the throne of that glory,
Jesus Christ,
to whom be honour and praise
through all ages. Amen.

Come, Our Lady, our only hope!
We beg you, illumine our hearts
with the rays of your grace.
Cleanse them
with the splendour of your purity.
Inflame them
with the warmth of your presence.

We ask you, Our Lady,
you who are called the morning star,
dispel with your light
the thick fog of allurements to evil,
which fill our souls.
Like the light of the moon,
replenish our emptiness,
and dissipate the darkness of our sins,

so that we may attain
the fullness of eternal life
and the light of never diminishing glory.
With his help, who made you our light,
and although born from you,
gave you life.
To him be honour and glory
from age to age. Amen.

Reconcile all of us to your Son
that we may attain
the splendour of his glory,
who at the annunciation of an angel,
willed to take his glorious flesh from you
and be enclosed in your womb
for nine months.
To him be honour and glory for all ages.
Amen.